The Neolithic Revolution

A Watershed Moment in Human History

In60Learning

CONTENTS

INTRODUCTION

The story of the Neolithic Revolution is our story and your story. It is the story of your great-great-great-etc-grandparents. It is the story of how our modern civilizations came about. Without the Neolithic Revolution, we would still be living in small tribes in the forest surviving as best we could on hunting and gathering.

However, this revolution did not happen suddenly. It took thousands of years to take hold. In general terms, the Neolithic period was characterized by sedentary farmers living in houses in small permanent communities. It was a very different lifestyle from the nomadic, small bands of human beings that characterized the Paleolithic, which is the way we humans had lived for hundreds of thousands of years before settling down as farmers.

Many historians consider this revolution to be the most significant period in the history of human development, as it laid the foundation for civilization as we know it. But it is only recently that archaeology, history, and a host of other disciplines have begun to uncover the full narrative of this remarkable period.

1 UNDERSTANDING THE STONE AGE

"My Oxford training was in the Classical tradition to which bronzes, terracottas and pottery (at least if painted) were respectable while stone and bone tools were banausic. [ED: meaning crude, not refined or sophisticated]"
V. Gordon Childe, The archaeologist who coined the term Neolithic Revolution.

On a field trip with her father during the autumn of 1879, the nine-year-old daughter of an amateur archaeologist let out a loud scream. "Dad, look, painted bulls!" She was holding a few candles and standing inside the dark Cave of Altamira in Spain. Her father, Marcelino Sanz de Sautuola, came to his daughter, Maria, and looked up at the ceiling. There above him were painted animals including the "bulls" his daughter had seen. The richly colored animals almost seemed alive in the flickering light of candles and the uneven rounded surfaces of the cave. He and his daughter were the first people to discover a full gallery of Paleolithic paintings. In his writings, De Sautuola said, "I was overcome with amazement. What I saw made me so excited I could hardly speak."

As a learned man and a dedicated amateur archaeologist, he came to these paintings with a wealth of knowledge. He had just seen an exhibit in Paris of Paleolithic objects and recognized that the paintings at Altamira were of the same style. And for years he had found a number of Paleolithic objects near the entrance to the cave, so he was reasonably sure the paintings were of the same period. To clinch his conclusion, he saw that the "bulls" his daughter had yelled about were actually bison, which had been extinct for thousands of years. So, with the help of a trusted and well-respected friend, Professor Juan Vilanova y Piera, he explored further and then published his findings in 1880. He wrote that the Cave of Altamira contained a wealth of paintings by Paleolithic people, cavemen, that were in almost perfect condition after tens of thousands of years. His findings were greeted initially with praise.

But, unfortunately, this story does not have a happy ending. Soon after publication, French Paleolithic scholars rejected his findings out of hand. They did not even go to the cave and look at the paintings. They said simply that crude, illiterate Paleolithic savages were incapable of making such sophisticated art. One very important French prehistoric art expert, Gabriel de Mortillet, led the chorus of criticism, even accusing De Sautuola of fraud and of having hired someone to fake the paintings.

This controversy lasted for a full 20 years, until 1902. During that time, De Sautuola died. Many think he died because of the attacks on his good name. Yet, finally, in 1902 his principal critic, Mortillet, recanted and wrote a quite famous mea culpa article in which he finally agreed the paintings were authentic, and further, that he had been wrong to accuse De Sautuola of fraud.

The really odd thing about this fascinating story is that learned men were blinded by their own preconceptions. They did not even go to the Cave of Altamira to look at the actual paintings. Their long-held belief that cavemen were only slightly more advanced than apes stood in the way of their understanding.

And there is another odd twist. Once one cave had been discovered, all of a sudden, a dozen or so other similar caves were discovered soon after. All of those caves with paintings had been there for tens of thousands of years, but no one had looked for them, or believed they were there. But once Altamira was found, people believed such findings were possible and began to look again at familiar landscapes, knowing that such finds might exist.

This article about the Neolithic Revolution starts with this story about the Paleolithic because the same misconceptions apply to the Neolithic Period. Until recently, in fact even today, many people assume that new stone age societies, Neolithic, were only slightly more advanced than old stone age societies, Paleolithic. But nothing could be further from the truth. The key watershed period in human history was the transition from Paleolithic to Neolithic.

A major part of this misconception is due to the way prehistoric societies have been categorized by modern scholars. The stone age period is two distinct and very different periods, but they are often lumped together. Furthermore, they are called stone age because they used stone age tools, but there was much more to their societies.

Paleolithic, or old stone age, used stone tools that were created by chipping off flakes until the tool was the right shape. This method is quite sophisticated and difficult for someone who is not familiar with the process. Paleolithic people lived in small bands, were hunter-gatherers, and were nomadic, meaning that they moved from place to place depending on the season.

For now, it is important to establish that human beings ten thousand years ago, fifty thousand years ago, or even two hundred thousand years ago were just as intelligent and just as skilled as we are today.

Anthropologists have stressed this point: that once we humans had evolved into Homo Sapiens, these people, our ancestors, hundreds of thousands of years ago, were just as smart as we are today.

They made the most of the technology they had and thoroughly understood the environment they lived in. Many anthropologists, when studying current hunter-gatherer societies, have noticed that these modern tribes have a comprehensive knowledge of wild plants, for example.

The paintings at the Cave of Altamira, created by Paleolithic peoples as much as 30,000 years ago, are a good example of the intelligence and sophistication of these much maligned "cavemen." While Altamira was discovered in 1880, it is only recently that the remarkable sophistication of the paintings has been understood.

First: The paintings have lasted tens of thousands of years. In comparison, paintings from ancient Rome only two thousand years ago are in poor shape.

Second: The paintings of the animals are realistic depictions. The images of the bison, for example, are clearly bison. The artists who drew these, painted from memory while they were deep inside a dark cave. This means these artists had remarkable powers of perception.

Third: The paintings are multi-colored, known as polychrome. The artists used a sophisticated "spray painting" technique. The paint was ground into a powder, mixed with animal blood, and then carefully blown onto the walls of the cave.

Fourth: The paint itself was powdered stone. In these paintings, these cavemen showed their thorough knowledge of the properties of stone and the way that paint would adhere and then remain on the stone walls of the cave.

What this means is that cavemen were very smart. And so it follows that people in the new stone age, the Neolithic, would build on that intelligence and be capable of remarkable achievements that many experts, only a few years ago, thought were impossible.

Yet, the exact transition from Paleolithic to Neolithic is not clear. It would also be a mistake to think that this transition from hunter-gatherer to Neolithic to Civilization happened everywhere, to all people. Today there are still nomadic tribes in north Scandinavia, for example, and settled subsistence farming villages that resemble the Neolithic lifestyle in China, India, Vietnam, Cambodia, Peru, and Mexico.

The Neolithic built its culture on knowledge learned during the Paleolithic. The late Paleolithic peoples had a basic understanding of planting and farming, for example. While it seems obvious to us today, it probably took thousands of years to figure out how plants grew from seeds and then how people could manage and control that growth. Some archaeologists have speculated that they saw plants they had eaten, grow magically from garbage piles where they had discarded seeds from fruits or vegetables. Eventually, they learned that plants came from seeds and could be "tamed" by planting.

In addition, Paleolithic cavemen had already domesticated the first animal, the dog. They knew how to skin animals and use their hides, and probably had a good knowledge of the night sky since they spent much of their time looking at the stars after the sunset. They also knew how to use materials in a complex way. One study showed that they used 22 raw materials and five different production stages just to make a bow, for example. So, the Paleolithic people had laid the groundwork for the Neolithic Revolution, and without their discoveries, the Neolithic cultures could not have occurred.

2 AN OVERVIEW OF THE NEOLITHIC PERIOD

"As the Neolithic was first defined in 1865, it was done without any regards to agriculture, sedentarism, pottery and all other innovations, now known to be associated with the Neolithic transition, but on the basis of the occurrence of polished stone tools."
R. Elburg, W. Hein, A. Probst and P. Walter
Field Trials in Neolithic Woodworking – (Re)Learning to Use Early Neolithic Stone Adzes

While the Paleolithic period lasted for hundreds of thousands of years, the Neolithic lasted about 8,000 years, from about 10,000 BCE to 2000 BCE. The Revolution occurred independently across the globe at roughly the same time. But keep in mind that different Neolithic cultures around the world began at different times and ended at different times, and new discoveries about the Neolithic period continue to be made today, so these dates could change.

While the term "Neolithic Revolution" was invented by V. Gordon Childe almost 100 years ago, the importance of this period has only recently been recognized as a crucial part of human history. If you don't know much about Neolithic civilizations and the Neolithic Revolution, you are not alone. College courses tended to gloss over this time period as simply an extension of the old stone age and then quickly move on to the first great civilizations, such as Egypt.

So how did this all start? Childe makes the point that many nomadic hunter-gatherer groups farmed, yet were not sedentary. The kind of farming they did was basic and seasonal. He called this simple cultivation, garden-culture or hoe-culture. For example, when a group settled down for a season, they might have cleared a bit of ground or used land cleared from the year before, thrown in some seeds, and then harvested before moving on.

It seems quite likely that some form of garden-culture was practiced during the transition between hunter-gatherer and year-round, permanent, sedentary, Neolithic farming. During the garden-culture period, people became increasingly familiar with farming and farming techniques.

At some point, when circumstances seemed favorable, they might have settled down to farm on a more permanent basis. Or, they may have started farming for a variety of other reasons. In one model, these nomadic people found that the climate of their hunting grounds had become much drier, so they settled near an oasis and began farming. Another model suggests that the game they hunted no longer existed, so farming became an alternative way to secure food. And in still another model, their hunting and gathering grounds may have been restricted by other tribes, so they settled near a river and learned to farm.

Childe imagined the following scenario about the transition from hunter-gatherer to sedentary farming in the Fertile Crescent in Egypt, one of the places we know the most about, and whose civilization is key to Western Culture. However, the following is only one example of how the transition may have occurred.

The climate began to improve around 11,700 BCE, when the ice age ended. The end of this glacial period meant that the weather was much warmer and wetter, as water, which had been absorbed by the glaciers, melted. This changed the overall climate, making it favorable for agriculture in some places. This is exactly what happened in the area known as the Fertile Crescent.

Childe said that the yearly and predictable floods on the Nile River meant that the land was both irrigated and also replenished with fresh new soil that the flooding deposited on the farmland. This area also had regular rainfall, so irrigation was not usually needed, but when it was, it could be easily added from the Nile River. And it just so happened that domesticated wheat from the area grew quite well in this kind of farm. In an environment such as this, a settled sedentary lifestyle made good sense and a good life for those involved.

So, it appears that farming and Neolithic villages took hold where the conditions were favorable. Then, as agricultural skills advanced, farming spread to other areas. As people learned more, these techniques could work in other areas where the initial environment had not been that favorable, but could now be engineered with irrigation and other methods.

Perhaps the most surprising fact about the Neolithic way of life, is that it sprang up all around the world at about the same time, even though these societies were not in contact with each other. The first Neolithic societies appeared in China, the Indus, Mesopotamia, Egypt, Ethiopia, New Guinea, Mesoamerica, and the Andes. And each of these may have had a different key staple crop that they farmed including wheat, barley, millet, maize, lentils, peas, flax, rice, yams, sweet potatoes, bananas, and sugarcane. Later, other crops were added such as beans, corn, olives, and grapes.

Also, although they had abandoned the Paleolithic nomadic lifestyle, they still retained many hunter-gatherer skills. So, they hunted for the wild game outside their small villages that they had carved out of the wilderness, and they fished and gathered wild plants to supplement what they grew in the fields.

Animals were domesticated about the same time as farming, and so the practice of animal husbandry began. As with agriculture, animals were bred for their usefulness to humans. During the Neolithic in Iran, for example, sheep were bred to improve and increase their wool. It appears that people generally domesticated those animals that lived in the wild in their areas such as sheep, goats, pigs, and horned cattle. In China the chicken was domesticated.

The principal innovations of the Neolithic Period were pottery, weaving, agriculture, and the invention of the wheel.

For archaeology, in particular, their pottery is important, as much of it has survived intact. While some early Neolithic cultures are considered pre-pottery, later Neolithic societies developed hand-made pottery, meaning pottery made by hand without a potter's wheel. Pottery is so important, that many of the Neolithic cultures are named for the type of pottery they made.

As best as we can tell, Neolithic societies were egalitarian, for the most part. Excavations of their villages do not show large differences in the size of their houses, for example.

It also appears that long-distance trading increased between communities. Materials such as obsidian for sharp knives and copper, were traded over a range of hundreds of miles.

Yet, domestic plants were key to Neolithic farming. Through DNA research, known in archaeology as archeoDNA, it appears that a major strain of wheat, emmer wheat, came from the Fertile Crescent, north of the Tigris and the Euphrates rivers, one of the birthplaces of civilization. This wheat had an unusual and critical quality for human cultivation. The seeds remained attached to the plant, rather than breaking off and scattering in the wind. In the wild, the normal scattering of seeds would be crucial for the survival of the plant. However, this wheat was ideal for human consumption, as the seed stayed on during a harvest, and so could be handled and processed easily.

It is estimated that these people had to save about a quarter of their crop every year for replanting. But when they did, these Neolithic farmers were able to select just the right seeds year after year from what they grew. Over time, the grain became much larger and had more nutritive value. In essence, they engineered their crops so that they were better than anything in nature.

Childe also pointed out that choosing wheat as a key crop was smart. Wheat had a number of properties, it was easy to store and did not go bad. In fact, if kept dry it could last for decades. This meant that the farmers could even plan for times of poor harvests by storing a surplus of grain after a bumper crop. But it had other advantages as well. Growing wheat permitted long periods when the crops did not need attention, which allowed for the production of other Neolithic items and the development of other Neolithic crafts. Wheat can also be processed in a variety of ways, making it quite versatile as a food.

The Neolithic lifestyle led to significant population growth. This would have been a problem for Paleolithic hunter-gatherers, as a large tribe would have to find more food and possibly exhaust the food that was available to them. But with farming, having more people to feed only meant that the farmland had to be enlarged. Children also were a benefit to the Neolithic lifestyle, as even very young children could help weed, for example, and help with farm chores.

With lots of food and time on their hands, it is likely that some specialization occurred, such as shoe making or tool making. It is also likely that ownership and property became important, and that society may have adopted a more stratified structure.

And with time on their hands, they created a number of mother goddess figurines. Thousands of figurines have been found throughout Europe and North Africa, and seem to be a central motif in their belief system, but more about this in a later chapter.

There were, however, important downsides. Occasional droughts or large changes in weather patterns could disrupt the agriculture, as could crop diseases or insect infestations. Since these farmers were now anchored to the land, they did not have the flexibility to move to a new location, the way they had as nomadic hunter-gatherers.

Sanitation was a problem as well, with people and animals living close together. It seems from archaeological findings, that disease was rampant. This was an entirely new problem, as closeness with a wide variety of people had not been a problem during the nomadic Paleolithic. And from the archaeological record, it appears that their life expectancy was shorter than it had been during the Paleolithic period.

3 NEOLITHIC HI-TECH

"After four field experiments, we can conclude that it is perfectly feasible to fell even large hardwood trees with copies of Early Neolithic adzes, as well as other Neolithic stone tools."
R. Elburg, W. Hein, A. Probst and P. Walter
Field Trials in Neolithic Woodworking – (Re)Learning to Use Early Neolithic Stone Adzes

As mentioned, the general perception has been that new stone age people were crude, unrefined, and barbaric; they were only slightly removed from the savagery of cavemen. In fact, one important anthropologist of the 19th Century characterized the transformation of human culture as "Progress from Savagery through Barbarism [i.e., Neolithic] to Civilization." Yet, as has been pointed out here, they were just as smart as we are today, in fact, as you will see, they may have had technologies that were better than even the Greeks or the Romans 3,000 years earlier.

The new stone age gets its name from its stone tools, which were smooth and polished. These signature stone tools distinguish the Neolithic, new stone age from the flaked tools of the Paleolithic, old stone age. Polishing was a remarkable advance in technology. By polishing the surface of the stone, which took a good deal of time, the tool was made much more durable. Given the right stone, the right grain of the stone, the right weight, the right balance, and the right form, a piece of stone could be shaped for long-term use and was unlikely to fracture the way flaked stones of the old stone age might do.

Modern researchers have only just realized that these tools were much better designed than previously thought. It turns out, they are good woodworking tools, for example. Since Neolithic people lived in houses, the tools they made were most likely designed to cut, shape, and carve wood, the wood they needed to construct a house. From post holes and rotten underwater wood remains, it seems clear that wood was a principle material, but most of it has been lost because it has decayed.

However, we do know something about their ability to work with wood. In 2012 researchers from the Freiburg University in Germany announced that they had successfully dated "the oldest known timber constructions in the world." This was a wood lining inside a well, radiocarbon dated between 5600 to 4900 BCE. The four-sided lining used complicated corner joints that fitted tightly together and has lasted underwater for 7,000 years. Using modern laser scanning, researchers were able to "read" the various marks the tools left, and understand how the polished stone tools were used to make the lining.

Another group decided to test the Neolithic ax and adze to see just how well they handled when trying to chop down a tree, for example. To their astonishment, these tools could fell a large oak tree. They also found that these tools handled quite well when it came to trimming the tree and shaping wood.

Also, it is important to note, that Neolithic people continued to use old stone age techniques when needed. For example, they used flint and obsidian blades shaped by flaking techniques when they needed a sharp edge, as polished stone could not hold such an edge. Obsidian is unique because it can create a knife that is sharper than today's best stainless steel scalpels used in surgery at a hospital.

Yet, their remarkable skills did not stop there. The new stone age people were the absolute masters of stone. Rather than thinking of their use of stone as primitive, think of it as the peak of stone technology. As you will see in the following chapters, they could quarry and shape extremely large columns of stone with stone tools, and then move these objects that weighed over 25 tons, 20 miles. And they could again quarry and shape five-ton stones with stone tools, move them 150 miles, and then set all of these upright in perfect alignment.

While the above example is from the well-known Stonehenge, there are at least 100 large megalithic structures across Europe. These used extremely heavy stones that have stayed in place for approximately 5,000 years.

In addition, Neolithic people created a number of very large stone buildings that are in good shape today. The 5,000-year-old Newgrange passage tomb in Ireland is made of stones carefully placed together without any mortar; it has never leaked in the wet climate of Ireland. Suffice it to say, these buildings, which are as old as the pyramids, are in very good shape considering their age.

Unfortunately, there is a huge amount of information that we do not know and can only guess, although we are getting better at understanding the missing pieces. For example, a Neolithic culture appears to have developed writing or proto-writing in the Vinca signs and symbols, a culture located in present-day Serbia. However, no one knows how to interpret them. We also know that there was proto-writing in the Gerzean culture that may have developed into Egyptian hieroglyphics. A 7,000-year-old Dispilio tablet of detailed symbols found in Dispilio, Greece, at a Neolithic lakeshore community, cannot be deciphered.

Probably most of the physical evidence for the Neolithic period is lost and unrecoverable. It is certain they had a sophisticated "weaving" technology, both for clothing and also in the sense of basket weaving and wicker construction. They probably made baskets, thatched roofs, fences, furniture, shoes, raincoats, and even boats out of reeds, cattails, rushes, willow, oak, and various grasses. We know, for example, that reed boats were made by the early Egyptians, because we have paintings of them. Otzi, the frozen corpse (mentioned next,) carried a woven grass cape that he used to keep the rain off. So, we can make an educated guess that they had this technology as well, since all of these items are still being made today by skilled indigenous peoples around the world.

And from the underwater find of the well lining, mentioned above, we know that artifacts may be in much better shape underwater than above ground. The Dispilio tablet had been underwater for thousands of years before it was found during a dry period when the lake level had gone down.

And there is the possibility that the intriguing new science, archeoastronomy, which combines archaeology and astronomy, will be proven at more Neolithic sites. If this is true, it might be an important part of the puzzle that helps us connect some of the dots with a new understanding.

There are also new ways of thinking about the astronomical purpose of Neolithic structures. For example, Dr. Fabio Silva at the University of Wales has suggested that the long passageways in a number of passage tombs in Portugal, that are all aligned the same way, might have been used like a telescope. By this, he meant that the passageways served as a kind of aperture which would darken the view of the sky and make citing certain important stars in twilight much easier. This was especially critical when viewing the star, Aldebaran, as it indicated the beginning or end of a seasonal period.

We now know for certain that some buildings are aligned with the winter solstice, such as Newgrange in Ireland. There are many more structures that may have an astronomical alignment, but cannot be proven yet. With computers, simulations, and laser scans, we might be able to decode this aspect of Neolithic culture.

The Neolithic story is ongoing. It is like a puzzle we are putting together and now, fortunately, we have many more pieces than we did before.

4 A NEW DISCOVERY AND NEW WAYS OF DISCOVERY

"Humans did not domesticate just other species; they also domesticated themselves."
David Christian, *This Fleeting World: A Short History of Humanity*

In 1991, while climbing in the Alps on holiday, two German tourists came upon a strange site. It appeared that part of a body was sticking out of ice in a gully. They assumed it was a hiker who had recently been caught and died in a snowstorm. But it turned out to be one of the luckiest and most important historic finds of the 20th Century.

The two tourists notified police, who tried to extract the corpse from the ice, but failed initially. A few days later, an expert team arrived at the site and began to suspect that they had found something remarkable. The corpse was almost perfectly preserved and was about 5,000 years old. He was from the Neolithic time period. Known as a natural mummy, he was older than Egyptian mummies that had been carefully dried and mummified, yet his entire body was wet and still intact.

Just as important as the body, was a slew of artifacts that this man wore or took with him before he died. The discovery was equivalent to finding an entire buried city like Pompeii, because the find was so complete.

Dubbed, Otzi the Iceman, because he was found in the Ötztal Alps, Otzi's body was moved to a permanent location, a refrigerated vault at the South Tyrol Museum of Archaeology in Bolzano, Italy where he is being studied to this day.

Otzi was wearing shoes, a hide coat, a raincoat over that, a fur hat, leggings, and belt and carried a pouch, a flint knife, a fire making kit, a bow, and a quiver of arrows, along with an unusual ax with a wooden handle and a sharp copper blade.

While Otzi's entire outfit was impressive, even more impressive was the sophistication of the materials used to make his various items. Virtually everything Otzi wore or carried utilized a variety of materials for maximum effect.

For example, his shoes were waterproof and appeared to be designed for walking in cold, wet weather, and the snow of the Alps. They were made of the following materials: the soles were bear-skin with its fur on the inside, the bear-skin was treated with bear brains and liver, the upper part of the shoes was made of deer-skin and tree bark. He even wore the equivalent of socks, which was a lining of soft grass inside the shoes. The shoe also had laces made from domestic cattle. The shoe design was so remarkable, a modern Czech company wanted to buy the rights to make and market a line of Otzi footwear.

The shoes are just an example of the sophisticated use of materials these Neolithic people of 5,000 years ago employed. Every item Otzi wore or carried was constructed with the same thought and care. For example, he wore a grass cape over his hide coat to protect himself from the rain. This design is still in use today in Japan. Woven grass is light and effective at keeping a person dry, since the rain does not soak in, but runs down the grooves of the weave.

Altogether, his clothing and tools utilized a wide variety of furs and leathers from both domesticated and wild animals. The domesticated materials included goat-skin and fur, sheep-skin and fur, and cattle leather and laces. The wild animal materials included deer-skin, bear-skin, and bear fur.

In addition to his clothing, Otzi carried a pouch that contained both a fire making kit of flint and iron to make a spark, and dry fungus to catch the spark, along with a birch bark container that kept a live ember. He also carried a sharp flint knife, a quiver of arrows, a bow, and two baskets.

Perhaps the most intriguing item he carried was an ax with a copper blade. While Otzi lived in the Neolithic, new stone age, it appears the Neolithic people were starting to understand the properties of metal as well. Otzi's copper blade was cast, forged, and sharpened. This late Neolithic period, that included some metal work, has been called the Chalcolithic, meaning the age of copper, but today it is generally considered part of the Neolithic period.

Yet, the discoveries gleaned from Otzi did not stop there. With modern DNA, x-rays, radiocarbon dating, and more, scientists were able to examine and are still examining his body and the various materials he used. For example, although copper mines existed near where Otzi lived, the copper for his ax came from central Italy, a distance of about 500 kilometers, or about 300 miles. This indicates that there must have been significant trade between distant Neolithic communities.

While discovering Otzi in such good condition with all his clothes and equipment was a remarkable find, equally impressive are the new tools that archaeology now has, to uncover the secrets of the past. Called archaeological science, the tools of this discipline have made our ability to reveal the past, much more powerful.

Radiocarbon dating:

Like the importance of DNA to forensic science, radiocarbon dating has revolutionized the ability to date old and ancient materials. Developed around 1950, it can accurately read the age of organic material up to about 50,000 years ago. This one technique alone has given science a firm way of dating many archaeological sites and materials. It has turned out to be much more reliable than even an expert opinion. Radiocarbon dating has taken the guesswork out of many finds, so, for example, it could confirm that Otzi the Iceman lived precisely between 3359 and 3105 BCE.

Aerial photography:

Quite a few significant indicators can be seen from the sky that cannot be seen from the ground. With the aid of photography, which can photograph landscapes with a variety of techniques such as infra-red, important discoveries have been made.

Drones:

In the past, hiring a plane has been very expensive. Now, with drones, it is possible to do aerial archaeological research that the archaeologist can control directly from the ground in real time.

DNA and ArcheoDNA:

It is often impossible to extract usable DNA from old material, but when it is possible, the results are significant. For example, as mentioned earlier, DNA was able to confirm that much of modern wheat came from emmer wheat in southeastern Turkey, not far from a major Neolithic or perhaps pre-Neolithic site.

Radiometric and other dating methods:

While radiocarbon dating works quite well for determining the date of Neolithic material, other forms of radiometric dating exist. Luminescence dating, for example, compliments radiocarbon dating, and in some circumstances, is more accurate, and can date material up to 350,000 years ago. When possible, it can provide a double check of a date determined by the radiocarbon method. It also does not require organic material, but it does require pottery or quartz that has been heated. Also, while radiocarbon dating has an upper limit of 50,000 years, another method called uranium-thorium dating reads dates from material up to 500,000 years, and can be used to help determine the time period of artifacts. This can be especially useful when a cave might have been used for tens of thousands of years, meaning that materials could have very different dates.

Combining methods:

As you will see, the existence and importance of the Goseck Circle was determined by a combination of two technologies: the aerial photography that located a ridge that was obvious from the air but had gone unnoticed for about 7,000 years on the ground, and radiocarbon dating that confirmed the photographs correctly indicated the site of a Neolithic structure.

5 ARCHEOASTRONOMY

"A good proportion of archaeologists and anthropologists have ignored the sky for too long, but the communities that built these prehistoric structures would have lived under dark skies and would have been inspired by it."
Dr. Fabio Silva, Lecturer in Skyscapes, Cosmology and Archaeology,
University of Wales

Before sunrise on December 21, 1967, Archaeologist Michael J. O'Kelly stood at the back of the narrow passageway inside the huge Neolithic stone structure known as Newgrange, in Ireland. He waited in total darkness. Then, to his astonishment, the rising sun slowly crept through the strange "roof-box" above the door, along the dirt floor of the long passageway, right up to where he was standing, and then the light receded until the hallway was completely dark again. O'Kelly said the sun was, "lighting up everything as it came until the whole chamber - side recesses, floor and roof six meters above the floor - were all clearly illuminated." O'Kelly later said he felt that he was among the gods of Ireland and that he could feel them around him as he stood there.

On that day, O'Kelly proved once and for all that Neolithic people were capable of accurate and sophisticated astronomical alignments, because December 21 was the day of the winter solstice. The odd "roof-box" acted like an aperture or a baffle to guide the sun into the passageway. But the roof-box was designed to do that only around the time of the solstice, and not any other time of year.

Just how O'Kelly figured all this out, is fascinating in itself. He knew that Newgrange was important to the Irish, as it was central to many ancient myths. Then, a number of local people told him there was a particular legend associated with Newgrange: that on an important day, the sun would reach to the back of the passageway and light the stone at the end of that hall. He thought at first that the locals must have confused this story with the possible solar alignment at Stonehenge. Yet, after hearing this story over and over, O'Kelly guessed that if it was true, the important day was probably the winter solstice. In addition, he needed to uncover the roof-box which had become overgrown. While he was not sure what to expect, he decided it was worth a try. Leaving his family just before Christmas, he drove the long distance to find out. Perhaps only an Irishman would have listened to local lore, lore which had been passed down for thousands of years, and taken it seriously. The result was a major discovery about Neolithic technology and skills.

Newgrange was built around 3200 BCE by Neolithic people, making it more than 5,000 years old, older than the pyramids and older than Stonehenge. It is part of a complex of buildings known as Brú na Bóinne, and it is not far from two other famous Irish passage mounds known as Knowth and Dowth.

Newgrange is only one of two undisputed Neolithic passage tombs that are aligned with the winter solstice. The other is Maeshowe in Scotland, which dates from around 2800 BCE, making it not quite as old as Newgrange. It was built in a similar fashion, with a passageway that invited the winter solstice sun down its corridor.

One researcher has suggested that the Newgrange alignment with the winter solstice was even more precise than originally thought. He suggested that the hallway at Newgrange could indicate the actual day of the winter solstice in real time, which is a very difficult calculation, and one that the Greeks and Romans 3,000 years later could not do. This could be easily proven with a computer simulation.

Both of these "passage tombs" are impressive and marvels of technology, but even more impressive is the fact that they are in good shape after about 5,000 years, and that they have continued to hold their alignment to the winter solstice sunrise. O'Kelly said, "I think that the people who built Newgrange built not just a tomb but a house of the dead, a house in which the spirits of special people were going to live for a very long time. To ensure this, the builders took special precautions to make sure the tomb stayed completely dry, as it is to this day."

Newgrange and Archaeoastronomy:

For the last 100 years, some learned men claimed that Stonehenge and other Neolithic monuments had celestial alignments. However, experts disagreed. The fact that there is now no dispute over the alignment of these two buildings, begins to settle this long argument. We can now say the Neolithic people were capable of engineering a sophisticated alignment. If they could do that, it is very likely they were capable of doing more, but this could be hard to prove.

Nevertheless, after much debate, the science of astronomy and ancient structures, known as archeoastronomy, has begun to come out of the shadows. Naturally, to be taken seriously, it needs to apply a rigorous methodology, which was too often ignored by enthusiasts. In addition, working with old sunken stones aligned to stars, whose alignment with the Earth has moved over the last 5,000 years, is a bit daunting.

The stars move a bit, but the Earth also moves over time in relation to the stars. This was known historically as the precession of the equinoxes, but is now called axial precession. In simple terms, the Earth wobbles over a 26,000-year time period, which changes the Earth's relation to the constellations and their stars. Nevertheless, with computers, these calculations are not nearly as daunting as they once were.

Now, it does seem that the long history of attempting to find celestial alignments with Neolithic structures is starting to take hold. This seems especially likely since computers can recreate the sky as it was at the time a Neolithic structure was built.

Here is a brief history of people who have devoted their lives to discovering how Neolithic structures were possibly aligned with the sun, moon, and stars.

The well-respected scientist, Sir Norman Lockyer, who discovered helium and who founded the journal Nature, and was its editor for almost 50 years, suggested that Stonehenge was aligned astronomically. He wrote the book *Stonehenge and Other British Stone Monuments Astronomically Considered* (1906; second edition, 1909), yet it was not taken seriously at the time.

The next person to suggest that these buildings might be lined up with the sun or the stars was Alexander Thom. Starting about 1955, he produced a slew of books right up to his death in 1985. But again, serious archaeologists ignored his work.

In 1965, Gerald Hawkins wrote *Stonehenge Decoded*. Using an IBM computer, which was new at the time, he claimed that Stonehenge was a kind of Neolithic computer that could calculate a number of celestial alignments and could be used as a sophisticated calendar for the sun, moon, and stars. While academic people did not take Gerald Hawkins' book seriously, and many of his assertions were disproved, it struck a chord with the general public, especially in the hippie 1960s and the new age kind of thinking.

This interest led to the creation of an academic position. Dr. Clive Ruggles was the Professor of Archaeoastronomy in the School of Archaeology and Ancient History at the University of Leicester, UK. Dr. Ruggles has written a host of reference books which form a solid foundation for further work in this field. He turned archeoastronomy into a discipline with an objective, rather than an emotional view. He has laid the groundwork for others to make further verifiable discoveries.

According to Wikipedia, there are almost 100 sites worldwide that are considered to have archaeoastronomical characteristics. Their actual alignment and purpose remain to be proven in most cases. But, with this many sites as candidates, it seems certain that some will yield new information about the Neolithic.

One area of interest deals with the phases of the moon and their relation to the solar year. Just about every advanced culture has tried to create what's called a lunisolar calendar. Farming communities especially needed to know when to plant and when to harvest based on the yearly cycle of the seasons, rather than the phases of the moon, which get out of sync with the solar year.

In addition, there are a number of celestial alignments and calculations that are not important to modern people, but may have been very important to Neolithic people. These are cycles and calculations that, we today, are not familiar with, such as the lunar standstill cycle, the Great Year or Metonic cycle, and the Saros (eclipse) cycle. The lunar standstill cycle is about the changing declination of the moon during an 18.6 year time period. The Metonic cycle is based on the fact that the moon's cycles and the sun's yearly cycles come into sync every 19 years. The Saros cycle is about the regularity of eclipses. All of these were known to the Babylonians as early as 2000 BCE, and it is clear that many Bronze age societies, the age right after the Neolithic, knew about these cycles and considered them important. So, it is likely that Neolithic people knew about them as well.

6 A GRAND TOUR

"There are more than a thousand passage graves along the Atlantic coastlands of northwest Europe. How they were used has been a question on the lips of many archaeologists for centuries."
Timothy Darvill, Professor of Archaeology at Bournemouth University

Take an armchair tour of the following places via the Internet. You will find good web articles on each one, but if you use Google Images (https://images.google.com/) you will see a host of photographs of each site. The places listed here are some of the most exciting, but there are literally hundreds more you can read about or visit. Neolithic sites go from Ireland to Turkey, in the West.

STONEHENGE
Stonehenge in England is probably the most famous Neolithic structure in the West, and is a UNESCO World Heritage Site. It has fascinated people for thousands of years and still does today, with new finds and new theories. It was one of the first sites to be excavated by archaeologists in the early 1600s. In 1906, the first aerial archaeological photographs in the UK were taken of it.

In the 12th century CE, an English cleric wrote that it was part of the King Arthur legend, in the 17th century John Aubrey, an early pioneering archaeologist, decided it was constructed by the Druids, who were in England at the time of the Roman invasion by Julius Caesar. And then finally, archaeologists realized that there had been a fully developed early civilization, the Neolithic, a civilization they did not know had existed.

With modern technology, the stone structure can now be dated properly. It was built in three major stages, starting in 3100 BCE, and ending about 1600 BCE. It is now generally agreed, that it is lined up with the winter solstice sunset. Also, there are a number of areas close by that

20

appear to have been associated with its use. In addition, there are large sites not far from it, such as Woodhenge, about 2 miles (3.2 kilometers) away, that were discovered with aerial photography.

During every recent decade, new excavations, new theories, and new findings have revealed more. For example, it now appears that 85-ton bluestones were brought from 150 miles (250 kilometers) to Stonehenge, in part, for their special acoustic quality. When struck, these stones make a distinctive noise. Some of the most current explanations echo the old ideas of the English cleric, Geoffrey of Monmouth, almost 1,000 years earlier, who believed Stonehenge was a place for healing, and also a place to honor the dead.

Stonehenge, however, is only one of a number of stone circles in the UK built during the Neolithic period. There are another nine major sites with large stones.

ORKNEY ARCHIPELAGO

The Orkney islands, in northern Scotland, may contain the most complete set of Neolithic structures in Europe, including stone circles, dwellings, a passage tomb, and large buildings for collective use.

A central area, known as the Heart of Orkney, is also a UNESCO World Heritage site. It includes Skara Brae, which is the most complete Neolithic town in Europe, as well as Maeshowe, which is a passage tomb, the Ring of Brodgar, and the Stones of Stenness, which are stone circles. All of these are on the main island of Orkney. Maeshowe is the only other passage tomb, beside Newgrange in Ireland, that all experts agree is aligned with the winter solstice.

Altogether, 25 family dwellings, in remarkably good shape, are found at the Knap of Howar farmstead, the Barnhouse Settlement, and Skara Brae.

Also, not far from the Heart of Orkney, is the Ness of Brodgar, which is a large six-acre area where excavations are now ongoing. The archaeological site includes a complex of large buildings that were probably used by the community as a group.

These ruins were only dated properly in recent years. After a major storm uncovered the stone village of Skara Brae, Gordon Childe, the leading Neolithic expert at the time, was called upon to study it. He decided, incorrectly, that Skara Brae had been constructed in the iron age. This shows just how hard it was to date things before radiocarbon dating. Fifty years later, radiocarbon dating determined that it was Neolithic, and 2,500 years older than Child had guessed. The entire area was built from 3600 BCE to 2400 BCE.

MALTA

For the Neolithic "wow" factor, the island of Malta, below Sicily in the Mediterranean, is the place to go. Seven temples are listed as UNESCO World Heritage sites, but there are more than a dozen additional sites on the island. The construction of the temples covers a wide range of time, from 5000 to 2200 BCE, or, from early to late Neolithic. These very old (some say the oldest) freestanding structures are made from well-crafted stone columns sculpted with stone tools. One temple, Mnajdra, is oriented to the summer and winter solstices, and to the equinoxes. It is a kind of yearly "clock," as a person can read the time of the year by the position of the early morning sun's rays on the clock.

The Hypogeum of Hal-Saflieni is an underground temple that was built around 3000 BCE and, may be the oldest such temple in the world. It is a completely underground structure with three levels, that connect via a maze of hallways, chambers, and steps. This temple has unusual acoustic properties. One central room was specially designed so that chanting there would be projected into all the other rooms of the temple. William Arthur Griffiths, author of *Malta and its Recently Discovered Prehistoric Temples*, wrote that a sound in this chamber, known as the Oracle Room, was "magnified a hundredfold and is audible throughout the entire structure."

GOSECK CIRCLE

Discovered in 1991, using aerial archaeology, photographs revealed a pattern of circular ridges in a field near Goseck in Germany. It became obvious that a circular structure had existed there some time ago. Upon closer inspection, radiocarbon dating placed the age of the post holes at about 4900 BCE. When the full design of the building was drawn, archaeologists realized that it was aligned to the winter and summer solstice. Pottery shards found near the site also indicated an age very close to that determined by the radiocarbon dating. About 120 other such Neolithic circular enclosures have been found in central Europe, but this may be the oldest discovered so far.

After the site was excavated, the old structure was reconstructed and opened to the public in 2005, just in time for the December winter solstice that year. It appears the enclosure was used both for ritual and for calendrical purposes.

DOLMENS IN PORTUGAL

View these megalithic dolmens on your computer and marvel at the different designs. They have lasted for as much as 8,000 years, while being exposed to the sun, rain, and wind.

In Central Portugal, there are a number of small Neolithic stone structures known as dolmens. These are situated on lower ground, and all point in the same general direction of the "Star Mountains." Naturally, people have wondered for years about their purpose, but recently a researcher believes he has found the answer. In the Carregal do Sal Nucleus and Star Mountain Range, researcher Fabio Silva located 23 small megalithic dolmens. Standing inside, these dolmens create a kind of telescoping and darkening effect when looking at the sky, making it easier to see stars at sunrise.

It is Silva's belief that they were designed as a tool to find the first rising of an important bright star, Aldebaran, in the modern constellation of Taurus. Known as the helical rising, this first sighting of a star was both a signal of a seasonal change and was also ritually important. In this case, sighting the star would have been a signal to leave the low ground and move herds of animals to higher ground. Silva tested this with a computer simulation and found that all were capable of sighting Aldebaran just before sunrise.

Take a visual tour of the Neolithic.

Copy and paste the following search queries into Google Images to see artifacts, buildings, figurines, pottery and more from the Neolithic era:

https://images.google.com/

neolithic Romania
neolithic Greece
neolithic Bulgaria
neolithic Serbia
neolithic Croatia
neolithic houses
neolithic tools
neolithic figurines
neolithic fertility figurines
neolithic art
neolithic pottery
neolithic Ireland
neolithic England
neolithic France
neolithic Germany
neolithic Spain
neolithic dolmens Portugal

7 ART, BELIEF, INVASIONS

"Old Europe was utterly forgotten until it began to be rediscovered by archaeologists in the decades around World War I. In that sense it truly was 'lost.'"
David W. Anthony, *The Rise and Fall of Old Europe*

In 1940, during the Soviet occupation of Lithuania, Marija Gimbutas was forced to hide in the woods outside the city where she lived because of her activities with the Lithuanian resistance. In the forest, Gimbutas worked on her Master's dissertation entitled *Modes of Burial in Lithuania in the Iron Age*. In 1944, Marija Gimbutas fled Lithuania with her Ph.D. dissertation under one arm and her baby daughter under her other arm, as she would later tell. Up to that time, she had survived the first Soviet occupation, and the following Nazi occupation of 1941, but felt she had to leave when faced with the second Soviet occupation at the end of the war.

It seems that Gimbutas had a story to tell and that nothing was going to stop her. Finally, in her 40s, she became the acknowledged expert on Neolithic Europe, especially the area she dubbed "Old Europe," which included parts of Greece, Romania, Bulgaria, and Northern Italy.

From childhood, Gimbutas had been steeped in the folklore, the pre-Christian cultures, and even the folk songs of Lithuania. Later, after getting her Ph.D., she was personally involved in a number of excavations. It is primarily because of her work and dedication, that people today have become interested in the Neolithic period in Europe, which had been ignored up to that time.

Through her research and archaeological digs, Gimbutas arrived at a number of ideas about Neolithic culture. Some were widely accepted and others were quite controversial. Yet, her conclusions were based on her vast knowledge and experience.

After personally finding hundreds of clay Neolithic female figurines, and then studying thousands more unearthed by different archaeologists, Gimbutas concluded around 1975, that in "Old Europe," and in many other Neolithic cultures, there had been a peaceful, egalitarian way of life that honored an Earth Goddess as their central deity, and that was a matriarchal society.

Soon, she was labeled a feminist archaeologist, which unfortunately changed the tone of the conversation. However, there was considerable evidence to support her ideas. One hundred forty-four female figures, known as Venus figurines, had been found at Paleolithic sites, dated from 35,000 to 11,000 BCE, so there had been a tradition of such imagery before the Neolithic era. At the same time, very few figures of men had been found. Robert Graves, the leading expert on Greek mythology, had written the book *The White Goddess* in 1948, and wrote that an early "Great Goddess was regarded as immortal, changeless, and omnipotent." In Greek mythology, a central Greek primordial Earth Goddess, Gaia, was the great mother of all the subsequent gods. And even thousands of years after the Neolithic, half of the Greek city-states honored a female goddess as their patron deity.

In any case, it is safe to say that a spiritual female figure was important to Neolithic societies.

Gimbutas had also claimed that the cultures of "Old Europe" were generally peaceful, and did not engage in warfare unless there was a compelling reason to do so. She was criticized for this, but her findings were at least partially true. A detailed study entitled *Warfare In The European Neolithic*, by Jonas Christensen, found that organized warfare and standing armies did develop gradually, but there were also regions where warfare was almost nonexistent.

In the year 1994, the French archaeologist, Jacques Cauvin, published his major work on the Neolithic in the Near East and the Levant. The book's title in English was *The Birth of the Gods and the Origins of Agriculture*. The basic theme was that the Neolithic Revolution involved a "Revolution of the Symbols," and that before the radical Neolithic changes in lifestyle could happen, there first had to be a major shift in thought. He argued that people began to believe in personified divinities that gave them power over nature. Because people identified with these gods on high, people felt removed from external reality and believed that these gods had given them both the right and the intelligence to control nature. This, however, came at a cost; humans now also felt a sense of alienation, a separateness from nature that was very different from their view of life during the Paleolithic.

In 1994, archaeologists made a discovery that seemed to confirm exactly what Jacques Cauvin was saying. A very old and complex site, named Gobekli Tepe, in Turkey, began to be excavated. Dated from the earliest times of the Neolithic, about 9100 BCE, this site showed a mastery of stone, with huge columns that had been shaped so they were smooth and straight. These columns are the oldest megaliths discovered to date. Yet, it appeared the site had been used by hunter-gatherers who perhaps came together for annual religious gatherings. In addition, the site had been used for thousands of years. The principal archaeologist, Klaus Schmidt, called it a "cathedral on a hill," and summed up his thoughts this way: "First came the temple, then the city."

British archaeologist Ian Hodder said, "Gobekli Tepe changes everything." But how our thinking changes, has yet to be determined. Gobekli Tepe is not far from the Euphrates River. The Tigris and Euphrates Rivers are considered one of the most important regions, where the Neolithic first took hold, and which developed into the first major western civilization of Sumer. In addition, Gobekli Tepe is not far from where the most important domesticated wheat, emmer wheat, grew in the wild. One theory about the rise of the Neolithic in Europe, is that it came from the Levant, the area of Gobekli Tepe, and led to the creation of the great civilizations of Sumer and Babylon, as it also spread into Europe over thousands of years.

While it appears that the Neolithic towns grew and evolved into the cities and civilization of Sumer, the same kind of developmental path did not occur in Europe. Marija Gimbutas theorized that an invasion of bronze age people who had domesticated horses and made extensive use of wheeled vehicles, had slowly taken over the Neolithic cultures in Europe. This theory is known as the Kurgan hypothesis. This model has been widely accepted, although modified a bit, and has been increasingly confirmed by DNA evidence. This "invasion" took thousands of years, altogether, and was not so much a conquering, as a takeover of Neolithic towns. Gimbutas believed that the egalitarian, matrilinear, peaceful, Neolithic cultures were overpowered by a militaristic, male-dominated, and hierarchical culture.

Evidence for some kind of major invasion or migration into Europe had been around for years. Linguists had noticed that there was a striking similarity to a number of words in various languages, languages that stretched from Europe to India. Dubbed Indo-European, a large number of linguists in the 19th century began to put together what might be the original language, a language they called Proto-Indo-European (PIE). And once put together, they began to make educated guesses about where the language originally came from. The theory now, is that the invaders spoke Indo-European and, eventually, that language became the dominant language in Europe, and it was also dominant in India and Persia.

From about 4500 to about 2500 BCE, experts suggest that Proto-Indo-European was spoken as one single language in Europe. Then it splintered into all the languages of today such as, English, German,

Spanish, Hindi, Persian, and French. Using the Gimbutas Kurgan hypothesis, it seems that the original invaders came from an area north of the Black Sea known as the Ukrainian steppe.

We hope you enjoyed reading this book as much as we enjoyed creating it. If you did, the team would greatly appreciate your feedback on Amazon or your favorite forum.

Please sign up for the LearningList at in60Learning.com to receive free ebooks, audiobooks, and updates on our new releases.

Happy reading!

The in60Learning Team

Made in the USA
Columbia, SC
16 September 2020

20752402R00021